T0337269

Jacky Newcomb is the UK's leading expert on the after-life, having dedicated her life to the subject. She is a *Sunday Times* bestselling author with numerous awards to her name, a regular columnist for *Take a Break*'s *Fate & Fortune* magazine, and is a regular on ITV's *This Morning*, and C5's *Live with Gabby*. Jacky has also appeared on *Lorraine* and *The Alan Titchmarsh Show*, among others.

Also by Jacky Newcomb:

From Angels with Love

From Angels with Love

True-life stories of
communication with angels

Jacky Newcomb

Harper
True *Fate*

Some names have been changed to protect
the privacy of the story tellers.

HarperTrueFate
An imprint of HarperCollins*Publishers*
1 London Bridge Street
London SE1 9GF

www.harpertrue.com
www.harpercollins.co.uk

First published by HarperTrueFate 2015

ISBN: 978-0-00-814449-4

Introduction

Do you believe in guardian angels?
Do you? I certainly believe! I've been studying the phenomenon of guardian angels for many years, and became particularly fascinated by the many real-life angel stories that appeared in my post bag from all over the world. I've written piles of books on the subject, including many containing true-life stories of angelic intervention. This is my favourite type of read, so I need no excuse to write another book.

I adore reading through your personal angel experiences and selecting stories for new books. This one is full of brand-new angel experiences for you, and I hope you enjoy reading it as much as I have enjoyed writing it.

If you'd like to believe that we each have our own guardian angel, but are not yet convinced, then these magical true stories may be just the thing. 'Magical' is a good word, because it shows that there is more to life than the logical. There is so much about our world that we don't fully understand, and people all over the world have seen, been touched by and even smelt (yes, indeed) an angel.

Angels intervene during challenging times. They have helped many thousands of people. Angels aren't just something from fairy-tales or fables; they are a real phenomenon and have been written about and discussed through many generations.

There are the angels we know from scriptures – religious books like the Bible and the Koran. Ancient scribes tried to classify and explain these mysterious beings of light. And even today, many volumes are written about them.

Over the years I've written my fair share of books and articles about them. I base my work on real experiences (both those I've had myself and stories from the many readers who've been kind enough to share their own angelic encounters).

Of these experiencers there are both believers and those with no real belief at all. You don't actually have to believe in angels to encounter one! Some people have been converted after an angel helped them – or even saved their life.

Like the Bible says, angels often come to us disguised. A random stranger may stop to help you at the roadside or appear when you are in distress. They seem to know things about you and talk about things that you haven't discussed previously with them. They are kind, loving and helpful. Most of all, people talk about how this 'person' appeared to them. It's common to talk about a 'person' with bright-blond hair and piercing blue eyes.

Their clothing might not seem to fit our modern-day surroundings or today's fashions. For example, one woman noticed that the man who helped her was wearing an old-fashioned knitted scarf and hat, even though it was a blisteringly hot day. Another pointed out that the woman who came to her aid seemed to be wearing beautiful clothes, but of a completely different era – a different time in history. Of course, it's common for people to wear retro clothing, but sometimes the person seems so different that they stand out from the norm.

Afterwards, it might be that other people didn't see the helper, or you turn to thank them only to discover that they have disappeared into thin air. These mysterious helpers regularly fade away, or we get distracted (or they distract us) so they can slip away unseen. There is often an air of mystery about the encounter, which leaves you forever wondering, 'What just happened there?' It might be much later that you go over the strange events of the day and only then wonder, 'Was that an angel?'

Other people tend to encounter angelic beings who look like the winged creatures of ancient lore, but this might well be during times of extreme stress. Maybe you are asleep when you see the angel, or unconscious, or your day-to-day life momentarily fades out as the angel appears to you. You might find yourself day-dreaming or your mind wandering. Your brain is quite literally in an altered state of consciousness.

Your state of consciousness can be altered by many different things: alcohol, drugs, tiredness or even just being hungry. By meditating we can make the change on purpose, and being alert and ready for action creates yet another state.

Our brains change state throughout the day, and there is some research that suggests high-amplitude delta waves (the Delta state: 0.5–4Hz) have been associated with the state of consciousness that people frequent when having a sixth sense or paranormal experience. This state is the one that also regulates human bodily function.

When the brain is passive it tends to fall into the Alpha range (8–12Hz), and it is in this relaxed state that many spiritual experiences occur. This is when many people see, feel, sense and smell angels! They also make contact during sleep (especially for me!). I often have angelic experiences while my body sleeps, but there is no mistaking these encounters for ordinary dreams.

I've known people to be 'put' into an altered state of consciousness. For example, someone might be going about their day, doing ordinary things, when all of a sudden the 'normal world' seems to fade away. They feel surrounded by a great feeling of peace and joy, as if they are connecting to someone (or something) else that is sharing this feeling with them. Sometimes they get a sense of whom, or what, is creating this energy (it might be an angel, or a recently deceased loved one coming by to say hello). They will probably see nothing (although they might see something), but the feeling is so strong, so real, they know without a shadow of a doubt that what they are experiencing is real, rather than created by their imagination.

Deceased loved ones (sometimes alongside angels) seem to 'create' the phenomenon so that they can communicate with us. This phenomenon can be used to give a deceased loved one the ability to announce to us that they have died before we can be told 'officially'. It's one of the many reasons they reach out to us.

Angels serve many purposes, including:

- Rescue work
- Healing
- Reassurance and comfort
- Announcing
- Warning

Maybe you can't see an angel but you sense them around you. You might feel a comforting hand upon your shoulder or a hand clasping your own. People say an angel encounter comes with a great sense of peace and calm. Your angel will leave you in no doubt that they connected with you. Inside you just 'know it was real', even if you can't prove it to others (assuming you'd even want to). Once you've connected with an angel, you never forget it. You'll know that angels exist and maybe, like me, you'll find they become part of your everyday life.

Just watch it doesn't create a lot of extra dusting. Dusting, Jacky? Yes! In my home I have angels everywhere – angel figurines, I mean. They sit on the sides of dishes, decorate plates and even hold the clock on my dining-room mantel. They remind me of my friend, the TV medium Colin Fry. One day (having recently been diagnosed with a terminal illness), he posted a message on his Facebook page. He thanked fans for their good wishes and healing but asked that they stop sending angels. Apparently his house was constantly full of feathers, which he was forever clearing up. I'm not sure if he was joking or not, but it made me laugh. Many fans had the same reaction as I did, and everyone was sending over angels to help this dear man in his time of need.

I also get a few white angel feathers of my own. Just this week I was talking about a deceased loved one. Knowing that my passed-over loved ones are with the angels can bring me such comfort, and as I got up to walk out of the room I stepped over a white feather. An angel had left me a classic sign, the calling card of the angels. It always seems as if they are listening in on our conversations (and, of course, they often are!).

Although I have a lot of angel figurines and angel-decorated items in my home, I know I don't have the biggest collection. Did you know that there is an angel museum in Beloit, Wisconsin? It's run by a lady called Joyce Berg in St Paul's Catholic Church (most of the collection once belonged to her). Joyce wears a silver angel costume when she works at the museum and admits to still having a very big collection of angels at home, too!

The museum currently houses the largest collection of angel figurines in the world at around 11,000. Joyce helped revive the church and now relies on donations to keep the museum running. The collection is most famous for the 600 black angels that TV presenter Oprah Winfrey donated. If you're close by, you might enjoy a visit.

But I digress. Let's explore a little more of the angel phenomenon.

From fairy-tale to true-life story
Here is a story you may have been told: every little girl and boy has their very own guardian angel. Your guardian angel's role is to take care of you and watch over you every day. Your angel is always close by in your time of need. 'He' (or 'she', or 'it' … for there truly is no gender) will rescue you if you need saving,

comfort you if you feel down and send you love and hugs if you need a little affection.

This is the story many of us are told when we are small ... if we are lucky; youngsters all over the world are taught that angels are real. Many of us are brought up with this belief, but when we reach a certain age, our guardian angel can disappear to the same place as the Tooth Fairy or Santa Claus. Your angel becomes designated to the 'myth pile'.

Yet I'm here to share a secret with you. Angels are real and they continue to exist ... and not just in your mind. They are real beings – beings of light, beings of a finer substance than the human body, but tangible just the same. Angels have interacted with humankind as far back as recorded history goes. Religious books are full of their collaborations with humankind, and many hundreds of thousands of people around the world today have experienced their presence.

So angels aren't just a legend from long ago. They work with humans even today, and proof of their existence lies everywhere. Regular readers of my books will know that I have shared many stories of my own. Although we all have angel experiences, many go unrecognised. As an author I record my experiences as they happen, and have learnt to respect the mystery and magic in my life. Sometimes I have several angel experiences all together; lots of things seem to happen so that I experience several paranormal things over the course of just a few weeks. Then I might go for months when nothing much happens at all. That is normal, for me. I've also recorded the true-life experiences of my family and friends.

Don't be fooled when I say these things are normal. What I mean is that I have grown used to them; I am now accustomed to the fact that the mysterious is a regular part of my life. I don't mean that I am so used to it that I take it for granted. Each experience is a miracle and I respect it as such. Recording these experiences by writing them down is a way of honouring that they happened. And then, of course, eventually they end up in a book – for these charmed encounters need to be shared!

Some lives are full of magic and yet others have nothing much happen at all. Naturally it's difficult to know if this would suggest that some people interact with angels all their lives and others are very much grounded on the earth plane – perhaps they are so focused on their earthly lives that they miss the mystical, even when it's right in front of them. I know that after reading examples of others' true-life stories, many of my readers recall unusual things that happened to them in the past.

Some of these behaviours may seem clichéd to you, but have a look at the list anyway to see if you recognise any of them.

- You feel an urge to travel a different way to work and then discover later that you narrowly missed an accident.
- You can't get the image of a person out of your mind and when you decide to call round to check on them you find they need help or have been trying to contact you.
- The same as above, but this time the image you hold in your mind is of someone who has passed over. Maybe you didn't know they had died, or perhaps you discover that it was the anniversary of their passing on that particular day, or their birthday. The 'coincidence' seems extraordinary (because, of course, it has real meaning behind it. One would call that synchronicity).
- You suddenly start worrying about your child. You rush to find them and discover they were in danger and you saved them just in time.
- Out of the blue you decide to check the insurance on your car, only to realise that the last date it's insured is ... today.
- You decide to keep some emergency cash in the house, only to discover you need it that very day.
- You decide to keep various items in the car in case of emergencies (a blanket and a shovel, for example, in case you get stuck in snow), and then need them later in the week.

You can ask yourself, 'Is this a coincidence, or was my angel urging me to follow a certain behaviour?' I felt the strongest urge one day to cancel my father's taxi service to the hospital for a routine appointment. Instead, I drove to his house and took him myself. As we left I gave him a long hug – it turned out this was my final opportunity to do so before he died.

Then a lady I know insisted her husband visit his cousin, who had been seriously ill. Although the cousin had seemed well on the way to recovery, she told her husband it was important he visit in case anything happened, warning him that he would regret not making the time to go. As it happened, it was their last meeting. Tragically his cousin died shortly afterwards. Did my friend's inner urging come from a similar source to my own? I expect this paragraph may have jogged your memory and made you think of similar experiences of your own. Most people have them from time to time in their lives.

I could keep on citing examples if I sat here long enough, but the point is, we've all had these 'coincidences' happen to us. Is it angels, spirits or a psychic connection we make with the other person concerned? Often (although not always) with angel experiences, there is a little added extra. Maybe two strange coincidences happen together, or a series of bizarre happenings coincide to save our lives, and we are left wondering how and why. Some people might call this a simple coincidence, but again, they are missing the magic. This is why I write things down; I like to see the patterns that occur.

Random people who don't know each other and may live on opposite sides of the world could have almost identical experiences. These people have never met, never shared their experiences (which may have happened many years apart), and the only connection between them is that at some point in their lives they shared their story with me! I thank God every day that people have trusted me with their angel experiences, because it is only through reading many thousands of encounters over the years that I have been able to learn, through patterns, what happens and why. But, of course, there is still so much more to learn …

Angel encounters come from far and wide. I currently live in the UK, and stories come to me from all over the country as well as all over the world. It fascinates me that similar stories might come from Japan, South Africa and Australia in the same month, from people who don't know each other, yet their experiences can be uncannily similar. This alone brings great magic. Angels interact with us in so many ways, but the incidences are not isolated or unrepeated.

- They can bring information we wouldn't normally learn until the future but which we need right now to calm and comfort us.
- They can bring a sensation of love and peace, which gives us a sense of well-being at times of great stress.
- They can bring us white feathers as a sign that they are nearby or to act as confirmation that everything will be okay.
- They might bring any number of gifts as signs that they are with us. Small coins are popular!
- They interact with humankind using music, scents, feelings and sensations or bringing signs of many different types.
- They can bring helpful people into our lives or alert us to things that will assist us.
- They can and do literally save human lives in the most unusual of ways – sometimes very dramatically.

Have angels helped you? I'm sure as you read through this book you'll recognise readers' stories, which may feel familiar to you or seem similar to experiences that you or your family and friends have been through. Angels' techniques do vary a little, but the end results are usually the same. It's important to them that we don't feel alone and that we know they are always around to help us – and help us they do.

Chapter 1

True-Life Stories of Angelic Beings

My sister Debbie recently got married in Cornwall, England. For those of you who aren't familiar with this part of the country, it's the gorgeous 'foot' of the UK; a narrow strip of land surrounded by sea and a favourite area for my family.

I lived in Cornwall with my husband for 18 months, and currently two of my sisters live in the county. I missed my sisters and this area of sandy beaches and fishermen's villages very much, so we've just moved back ourselves. The trip is a long one from our old Midlands home. In theory, it's possible to do the trip in around four and a half hours, but it's inevitable that at least one stop (usually three) and various roadworks mean the trip is often six to seven hours or more.

Our drive to the wedding was fairly uneventful, the wedding itself was small and memorable (in a good way) and the sun came out even though it was December. My favourite photograph is one of my mum Maggie, the bride Debbie and myself with my sister Madeline (my co-author on another book). We are standing on the balcony of the hotel with the bright-blue sea in the background. It just sums up the wedding completely! It was wonderful.

We knew there had been heavy snow higher up the country and were a little worried about our return trip. The day came to say goodbye; we were travelling home at the end of 2014, just a couple of days before the New Year, and although we were up early, because we were all staying in different places it took a while to say goodbye to everyone. When we set off on our journey, the sun was shining again and we were feeling fairly optimistic.

We had a car-full. My husband John and I sat in the front; my daughter, granddaughter (nearly 4) and mother (almost 80) were in the back. We'd already made three toilet breaks when we began to hit snow. It was falling gently, so we didn't panic as we left the motorway café, but less than a mile later the car began to shudder. My husband slowed down and pulled over to the hard shoulder on the road. It was getting dark. He popped open the bonnet – there was no smoke, but it was difficult to see what was wrong, with the light now poor. In any case, my husband was not a mechanic and really only knew the basics of car maintenance (much more than I knew myself!). He closed the bonnet and tried the ignition, but the car wouldn't start.

I looked out of the car window. It wouldn't be safe to stay sitting in the car with the fast traffic going by and poor visibility, yet the alternative didn't look any better. How could I ask my elderly mother and young granddaughter to stand on the embankment in the snow and dark – I noticed that the grassy area sloped away sharply, creating another potential hazard.

I prayed; there was nothing more I could do. *God ...? Archangel Michael (the protector angel) ...? All of our angels and spiritual guides ...? Deceased loved ones ...? We need you now! Please. We need to get the car home with all the passengers safe.* I knew that my husband would be able to sort out the car sometime during the following week; we just needed to get home.

Please, could you help us? I begged in my mind. I appeared calm, yet inside I was terrified, now trying hard to keep it together and not frighten our passengers. We needed to be somewhere safe, and fast. The side of the motorway in the dark and poor weather was not where I wanted to be.

My husband turned the key again and this time the car started immediately. The warning light that had appeared on the dash a few minutes earlier had switched itself off, but as we were still two hours' or so drive from home we decided to find somewhere safe to park and then call out roadside assistance to get it checked; we drove slowly off the motorway.

The next exit was less than a mile away and I spotted a signpost for a pub with a large car park. 'Pull off there!' I yelled to my husband, and he just managed to coast the car into the car park and into a parking space. I gave a silent word of thanks to the angels and shuffled my daughter, granddaughter and mother into the pub where we sat in the warm, drinking coffee; the little one drinking a juice box.

As we were members, my husband called out roadside assistance. On the phone he was told we could have a three-hour wait and none of us were surprised; it was holiday season, after all. It was their busiest time of year, they said, and many cars had broken down. At least we had somewhere nice to wait – I was grateful for that. I noticed that at the other side of the car park there was a small hotel. *Could be useful*, I considered, and felt reassured!

Three minutes later my husband's mobile rang and he shuffled away outside to get a better signal. Then he came back with a smile on his face. Our Jaguar car was going to be looked at by an engineer who was on his way home. He was moments away from our location and – you'll never guess – he was a Jaguar specialist! What were the odds of that?

No sooner had my husband drunk his coffee than his phone rang again. It all happened so quickly. The engineer was outside waiting, and I have to admit that as my husband went outside in the cold I was grateful to be snuggled up in a comfortable chair inside! Ten minutes later my daughter went outside to check on the progress. Apparently we had a split radiator pipe and the engineer was able to make a quick repair. It would get us home safely and we'd easily be able to sort it out the following day.

One minute we were breaking down on the side of the motorway and the next we were driving home. The whole thing had happened so neatly, so swiftly, almost as if someone or something had intervened. But, of course, I had asked for angelic assistance. Another of those useful coincidences, do you think? The rest of the journey was uneventful – just the way I like it. The following morning my husband went to get the car fixed properly; the pipe cost just £4!

Did angels intervene in our journey? Did they set out to rescue us as I'd asked? We'll never know for sure, but we all realised that things changed after I'd asked for angelic assistance. Can you imagine what it would have been like to have stood in the dark in the cold and snow? We all had the residue of colds, and my mother had been suffering from bronchitis for several days. The situation could have been serious for her – fatal even – but luckily it wasn't.

I particularly loved that the repairman was so close by. A three-hour wait would have been equally as challenging. My little granddaughter was already exhausted from the trip, but in the end the short break in the warm pub just refreshed her as she snuggled up on my lap. It was actually rather nice.

My life is full of such examples of mysterious assistance. This time the help wasn't dramatic, but it was welcomed. I've written about it in numerous books. While I'm not suggesting the repairman himself was an angel, everything came together rather neatly after I'd requested angelic assistance. Have you ever tried something like this?

It's not just me, of course. Thousands and thousands of people have shared their stories of angelic or perhaps divine interaction. One thing we know for sure is that there are far more things going on in our world than we can even begin to explain. That won't stop me from sharing these stories with you. Have you ever been through a rescue situation like this? Or experienced strange and unexplainable circumstances that have helped you safely on your way? You need never feel embarrassed about it – many people have.

I've written many books that include strange and paranormal experiences of my own. I've had help on car journeys before. I once heard angelic voices bring me a warning message when I was driving: *stop*, *pull over*, it told me. It prevented me having a head-on collision. I've been rescued from the sea – saved from drowning – and been given important information when I've needed it most. Mainly, angels have reassured me when I've been worried, or comforted me when I've been grieving. They seem always to have been in my life. I've shared all these stories, and many more, in my other books.

Angels have always been in your life, too. You may not know or recognise it when they are around, but when you read other people's stories you will recall your own. That's the wonderful thing about it. You'll remember those occasions when something strange (or wonderful) happened, and at the time you were aware of it but then pushed it to the back of your mind. You'll know that when life is busy we don't always question those things; we're grateful, relieved even, but then we get on with our busy lives. Angel experiences are like that! They sneak in when you least expect them and then disappear again, leaving you wondering.

Some of the more unusual angel encounters have involved helpful strangers who appear in unexpected ways. They might approach you as a stranger, but whisper words that change your life. Sometimes this unfamiliar person will talk to you about a situation they know nothing about. For example, you might be crying on a park bench because your dog has just died and your new companion will come over and say, 'Don't worry, your dog is now in heaven with the angels …' – that sort of thing. Although you feel wonderfully comforted by their words, it's only later that you realise you didn't know the person and hadn't told them about your pet.

Sometimes these beings will appear in dreams; most of my own experiences happen this way. An angel (not looking much like the angels we're familiar with) will visit me in a very realistic 'dream' or visitation experience. They pass on words of wisdom or reassurance, rather like life lessons. When I wake up after such an encounter I am always calmer and happier about my situation. On occasion I've been woken from a deep sleep to hear a voice call my name. Sometimes the voice is unknown to me, but other times the voice may appear to belong to a deceased loved one or friend. Either way it brings comfort. Have you ever heard a voice call your name or had a powerful dream with a message?

It happened just this week. I actually woke up because I heard my own voice say, 'Yes?' in reply to someone calling me. A couple of days later I visited my mother, who told me she had woken in the night. She thought she had heard her late partner Brian calling her name (as he often did when he was sick). She was confused when she woke and remembered that he had died. The next morning she realised it had been 12 months since he'd passed – 12 months to the day! Perhaps Brian had practised on me two days earlier! Was it him (or the spirit of him)? Or maybe it was an angel letting us know he was okay. Perhaps it was just a coincidence, as many people say. But in my life, at least, 'coincidences' begin to add up!

Sometimes these visits have life-changing purposes. For example, 46-year-old Beth Peterson wrote an extraordinary book about how she was struck by lightning ... twice. The odds of this happening even once are apparently 300,000 to 1. In her book, *Life After Lightning*, I was especially interested in what happened after she was hit and died. Beth says she knows it sounds crazy but she remembers being taken by angels, up and away from her body. She was given a choice (by God) to either die at that moment (in other words, not go back to her body) or come back to earth and help others who have also been through trauma.

During the whole experience she felt completely at peace, and although she felt ready for her life to be over, she felt that there was more she could do on earth. Beth decided to come back into her body and recalls that she felt as if she were being squeezed into a jar as her soul 're-entered' her body! Her experience was very traumatic, but she was greatly comforted knowing that there is life after death.

Donna Ferguson had her angel experience shortly after giving birth. She eventually went on to share her story in the Sky Real Lives TV programme *Angels*, back in 2009. Her pregnancy had been normal, but after the birth she was exhausted and a little faint. She was losing more blood than was usual, but hadn't realised at first that there was anything wrong. To help her sleep a nurse took her new baby to the nursery, and Donna soon drifted off. It was then that Donna heard a voice urging her to wake up. The young woman argued with 'the voice' and kept repeating that she was too tired and needed to sleep. The voice persisted, telling her to press the alarm lying next to her, so she did.

Donna was lying in a pool of blood and was immediately rushed to theatre – she needed an urgent transfusion. It turned out that a large part of the placenta had been left in the womb. Shockingly, she had been close to death, but went on to make a full recovery. Reflecting on her experience later she feels that angels intervened and saved her life by keeping her awake long enough to summon assistance. Donna knew she wasn't meant to die that night; it wasn't her time. I know that her partner and five children would agree!

I wrote my first angel book many years ago. It was published back in 2004. Since that time people have read my books and continued to send me stories. You know experiences are real when you hear such similar tales from around the globe. Many people discover my books through coincidences. Maybe they have been talking about angels to a relative and then out of the blue a friend offers to lend them a book on this very subject. Maybe my books have been recommended to them, but then someone else randomly buys them one as a gift. I've heard some extraordinary stories about books that have flown off shelves at people's feet in bookshops and libraries (potentially dangerous, but luckily divinely delivered).

Other people have told me that psychics have passed on my name or that I have personally appeared to them in dreams (I wish I remembered those!). I might have given them words of wisdom or appeared with angels to communicate with them. It sounds awesome, but I recall none of them. I guess it's some higher aspect of myself that partakes in these magical journeys, certainly not the everyday part of me that loads the dishwasher and cooks dinner. If only the normal 'me' was so wise and angelic! ☺

I do believe these experiences have been brought about directly by angels. When the student is ready, the teacher will appear, they say. Many might initially feel that anything to do with the paranormal (above and beyond normal) or the occult (the unknown) is potentially frightening (or indeed terrifying). Yet nothing could be further from the truth. Angels bring such love, great wisdom, kindness and caring. They protect us from harm, they calm and guide us and even save lives. You only have to read just a few of the stories in my books to know that we are dealing with a very real and wonderful phenomenon – divine help from angels with love.

These days, I do select the more unusual or dramatic experiences for my books. Yet thousands upon thousands of people find a simple white feather (an angelic sign) in times of need, or maybe just feel a gentle touch when they need reassurance. Perhaps for you the experience was even more subtle. Maybe an angel simply brought you a feeling or sensation that they were around, making you feel calm instead of frightened or unhappy.

Having said all of that, these dramatic encounters still happen to regular folk. You don't have to be a saint or a religious person to encounter angels! Many of the more dramatic angel experiences do happen during major life experiences. You might be more likely to see an angel at a time when your life is at risk, or you are unconscious or asleep, as we discussed earlier.

Angels find it difficult to make themselves known or seen during normal waking hours. Our human eyes are just not equipped to perceive them during this state (but the angels do still keep trying!). Therefore their interaction can seem mysterious to us, magical even. When they seem to break the laws of nature as we know them, their interaction seems unearthly. Imagine, now, showing a modern-day mobile phone to people of the Victorian era? Could they even get their heads around the idea that a three-year-old child could use such a piece of technical equipment? When I was a child my uncle Eric had the first calculator that was mass-produced. As kids we stared in wonder at this magical device that worked out the sums you couldn't easily do in your head. He'd spent a small fortune on his calculator, but now of course you can buy them in the pound or dollar store! Are angelic interventions simply science we don't yet understand? Does it seem so strange because we don't understand it and can't scientifically work out why it happens and how?

The way that angels move between dimensions is a science we haven't worked out, but it doesn't mean these things don't happen – they do. Angels seem to appear rather suddenly and then disappear again the same way. Many people find it hard to believe that such things exist in our modern-day world, but those who have experienced the phenomenon have no doubt that angels are real. In years gone by, people believed that angels must need wings to travel. We still use images of angels with wings to represent these creatures, although these days we understand that 'wings' don't help much with inter-dimensional travel! People still talk about their angel experiences in the way they did in ancient times. It happened then, and it happens now.

Beth (the lightning lady) Peterson's first angel experience happened when she was around two and a half. At the time she had a severe case of whooping cough with fevers and vomiting, which she remembers as being very frightening at the time. She knew how worried her parents were – she could feel their fear. Her mum would add water to a pink powder that Beth would then have to drink to get better.

Her dad slept with Beth on the bathroom floor on the blankets they had laid out for them both. She recalls that they slept on the floor for many days. She remembers so many things from this traumatic time in her life, but most of all she recalls the angel. The first time Beth saw the angel she was hovering in the corner of the bathroom, then floating above her, smiling and singing. Occasionally the angel stretched down and touched the youngster, and Beth felt frightened that the angel might take her away with her. Luckily she didn't.

The kindly figure had long golden hair and bright-green eyes; her skin looked soft and the little one longed to touch it. The angel's robes were a mixture of blues and flowed down beyond her feet, while her songs sounded so caring and loving. Beth felt that the songs had a type of healing quality to them, as if the songs themselves made her well again. As she began to improve, the angel just faded away. Beth believes that the songs were meant to calm her, but she also thinks they had a healing vibration to them, a special type of energy that was being directed at the little body on the floor below. Years later, she still felt that the singing was how the angel made her well again.

As the days passed, the being's beautiful light faded away and Beth just resumed living life. Yet she never forgot the beauty and serenity of what she had experienced. At many times during her life, she reflected back to that moment. But then the proof of its truth (had she ever needed it) was thrust in front of her in the most dramatic way. In July 1992, as Beth was struck by lightning, she felt herself (her spirit) being lifted from her body and taken to the other side of life. There she was shown her life so far, and just moments into the viewing she was shown the bathroom where she'd been so ill. The angel was with her in the scene, singing to her as she remembered. It was at that moment that she realised the very same angel was standing right next to her during her near-death review in heaven. The angel hugged her 'with her heavenly glow', and Beth thanked her for taking care of her during her childhood illness.

Beth says she was elated to have heavenly confirmation that her memories were accurate, and she believes that angels really do exist in our lives during our moments of need. You can read more of her lightning-strike experience in her book, *Life After Lightning*.

I love that Beth's earliest memories of angelic contact came from a childhood experience. I've had lots of letters about childhood encounters with angels. The son of a family friend talks about his angel 'Mike' all the time. He is five and can see his guardian angel very clearly. Mike is funny and often gives the young boy important or unusual family information ahead of time, to his mother's bewilderment. One day he told her that my daughter (his mum's friend) had hair like a mermaid, in green and purple – angel Mike had just told him and it made him laugh. As unlikely as this sounds, it was true! A few days later when the friends got together my daughter showcased her new 'do' in just these colours (she usually has it pink these days!). Isn't that funny?

Dr Melvin Morse specialises in afterlife experiences following near death. In his book *Parting Visions*, Dr Morse says his research shows that around 50 per cent of children who've had near-death experiences see angels. So it's quite common in children who have been through trauma.

Donna saw angels during her own near-death experience, although she was an adult at the time. A doctor made a mistake while Donna was undergoing surgery. Donna immediately felt herself lift up and out of her body, and two angels then appeared to take her 'home'. They told her they were escort angels and their role was to guide her to heaven. She was taken to a place where she was able to ask questions about her life and others who had shared it with her. She felt great joy during this awe-inspiring experience, but soon became aware of doctors working on her body below. Donna felt she was given the choice of whether she should live or die, and as she chose life, she found herself back in her body once more. The angels disappeared in front of her by flying through the wall!

Angels are around to protect, guide and watch over us, and to keep us well and healthy when they can. Clearly, having a bit of fun is not beyond their remit. I think they believe that we take ourselves too seriously. Life is a series of lessons, like in a big classroom. Angels often remind people to enjoy themselves more. They must think us silly when they look at the things that seem important to us.

Who among us hasn't worried that they don't have a perfect outfit to wear to a special occasion, or hasn't got upset because they are having a bad-hair day? I sometimes get cross because I have no chocolate in the cupboard, or because I wanted to buy some frivolous thing for the house and couldn't afford it. I know my angels want to give me a good shake on occasion – what about yours? Their message usually points me in the right direction – to the fact that the most important thing we should be doing is loving one another. It really is that simple!

Chapter 2

A Little Bit of Love

Love is the strongest message that angels can bring to us. It's our most important life lesson: to love, to be loving, to receive and accept love. Sean's experience was also gentle and loving. Was an angel at work in this case? He told me that a couple of years ago, he was photographing a family friend's wedding. It was 21 June, the summer solstice, so you'd think it would be a fantastic day, with the sun shining, but no! It was dark, and rained throughout the day.

The hotel where the young couple got married was located right next to the beach, and the bride and groom wanted photos on the stretch of long sand. They walked down the approach ramp to the seashore, but the rain just got heavier. If ever there was a need for angels to intervene, this was it. The photographer told me that as they were about to turn back to the hotel without the desired images, a young girl appeared from nowhere and asked his assistant if they would like to borrow her umbrella for the bride and groom.

From Angels with Love

Sean said he was delighted. The umbrella was see-through with pink hearts on – what a fantastic tool! Sean says they got some fantastic photographs that couldn't have been designed any better. He believes his angels were working overtime that day for sure! Sometimes the angels bring helpful people to us just like this. Angel experiences can be very dramatic, but they don't have to be. This gentle encounter was filled with love, and there was nothing spooky about it at all.

Sometimes it's the little details that count, like in Eileen's experience. The poor woman was involved in a head-on collision in her car on her way to work. It was, she says, a cold, cold day. Trapped in her vehicle, she called out for help. Suddenly a man appeared and passed her a blanket through the window, which really calmed and comforted her ... as well as warmed her! He reassured her that the paramedics wouldn't be long. Eileen had to be cut out of the car and it took some time for the work to be completed; all the time she felt safe under her blanket. Paramedics strapped her to a stretcher and she asked to speak to the man who'd brought over the blanket. 'Blanket?' the paramedic asked, confused. There had been no blanket and, even stranger, no man! At least, none visible to anyone at the scene but Eileen!

These types of experiences are typical of angelic encounters. The mysterious stranger who appears and then disappears again once help arrives. Many people recall the kindly voice or the hand that held theirs while they were waiting for help. During trauma, when people's other senses fade away, hearing often remains. To hear a voice telling you that everything will be okay is truly the difference between life and death in many cases. It seems that this is the time that angels come into their own, doing their thing and taking care of people in the gentlest of ways.

Sally's story is the perfect example. When Sally was six years old, like most children she was frightened of the dark. The worst time was the long walk down the corridor from the bathroom in the middle of the night. On the way back from the bathroom one night Sally heard a noise and froze. The youngster was so scared, but then suddenly her 'mum' appeared and took hold of the little one's hand, and together they walked back to the bedroom. Yet when they went back to the bedroom, they passed her mother's bedroom and there in front of them, fast asleep on the bed, was her mum! How could this have been possible? Now an adult, Sally believes that an angel appeared as her mum that night to keep her safe and reassured.

Lucia wrote to me and shared this lovely little experience. One day during the winter her son Alex took his phone to school. During his lunch break the young boy accidentally dropped his phone somewhere on the field when he was taking his gloves out of his pocket. When his mum picked him up from school he was disappointed at losing the phone, but worse still, it was the beginning of the school holidays. A week away from school would mean that the phone would probably get wet and therefore ruined by the weather.

That evening Lucia called out to the Archangel Michael to help. Could he? It was worth a try. Michael is the angel we know the most from the Bible, and some would argue that he is the best known of all the angels. Could Michael help to find the phone? Michael's primary role is protection, but he's also associated with finding lost things.

Then a week later the children went back to school and at home time Alex came rushing out with the phone in his hands. Rather strangely, a friend in another class had found the phone on the field that day. Even though the weather had been so bad during the week's holiday, the phone was working perfectly. Even more strangely, the school friend's name was … Michael!

Some of these experiences appear to be coincidences, and I think that is the point. These subtle interactions change lives. So far this chapter has shown a selection of gentle and even fun angel-inspired stories. The following experiences also happened to real people, but not all of them are so subtle.

This next story seems extraordinary and was reported on the TV news in Spanish Fork, Utah, and around the world. Eighteen-month-old Lily was hanging upside down in her mother's car after a crash that had happened the night before. The car had ended up in the icy river below. Lily's 25-year-old mother, tragically, had not survived the accident.

Yet even though the mother had passed on several hours earlier, four police offers who were called to the crash 18 hours later, after the car had been spotted, could hear a woman's voice in the river below, calling out, 'Save us!' Initially people were unsure if anyone was in the car, but the voice urged them forward to where young baby Lily was found.

It seems the voice of Lily's mother may have carried over from the other side of life. Was it the spirit of the young mother calling for rescuers to save her little one, or was it angels, somehow directing helpers to lift the baby from the icy waters? Perhaps we'll never know. One thing is for sure: those police officers have a mystery they will carry with them for the rest of their lives. When interviewed by the television station they all looked moved by their experience, and when I first heard of this story it gave me shivers!

Has anything like this ever happened to you? An unexplained voice directing you to take one path over another? Over the years I've had many people write and share such stories. Sometimes unexpected events might stop them from being in a certain place at a certain time. A building collapses, a murder takes place – it's shocking, but true. Angels (or a mysterious unseen presence) seem to guide us away from danger, or, as we saw in the story before, lead rescuers to our side.

If there is one thing I have learned, it's that life is not as straightforward as we imagine. Human beings are logical creatures, yet the world around us is not. Our world is full of the mysterious and the unexplained; there are books full of such stories (and television programmes dedicated to trying to explain them). To have an open mind seems the most helpful approach. We might not understand everything that happens around us, but does that even matter? Do we need to understand magic to be affected by it in a positive way? It seems not!

As the years have passed, I've recorded most of my own psychic experiences in my books, magazine column and features. My family have given permission for me to record their stories, too. I am lucky in that my books have reached hundreds of thousands of people around the world, but I consider it my life mission.

Why not keep a record of your family's miracles and angel experiences as part of your own life mission? I bet if you chatted to relatives you'd find lots of supernatural and unexplainable stories. It would be lovely to keep your notes in a book or binder bought specially for the purpose, or perhaps to start recording your encounters on the computer or by voice recording. It would be a wonderful gift for future generations. Don't think of it like writing a book (you'll feel overwhelmed if you do); just jot down the details – the basic outline of the story, when it happened, to whom it happened, and maybe how their life was affected by the experience, both at the time and afterwards. Who cares about spelling? (If I'd worried about my own terrible spelling, I'd never have written any of my books!) Just jot down those notes!

Begin with yourself. Did you ever find a white feather after asking for help? Did you ever hear a favourite song after asking for help from a deceased loved one? Perhaps a light flickered as you asked about angels, or a friend appeared unexpectedly at a time when you were in trouble. Have you experienced mind-to-mind contact with the living or the dead ... or even angels? Of course they hear us, and then they put into action the assistance we need. Have you ever felt an angel or a deceased loved one draw close to you? Did you ever smell a strong flower scent that seemed to come from nowhere? Did a deceased loved one appear to you in a dream? I bet you've had many experiences and simply put them to the back of your mind.

I firmly believe that when you record (with grateful thanks) the experiences of miracle happenings in your own life, you draw more towards you. By recognising the ones that have gone before and acknowledging the most important of spiritual experiences, you become open to many more of the same. Fingers crossed!

Chapter 3

Children's Stories

When angels appear as real-looking people it can sometimes be more helpful. Betty was bullied from a very young age by one person in particular. She says her parents never believed her and she was a very shy person and found it difficult to cope.

There was one occasion that does stand out in her mind and she shared it with me. She tells me that when she was 12 years old and was walking home from school one day this girl was behind her with one of her friends. The whole way home the girl kept pushing Betty in the back and threatening to take away her toys and friends. She terrified Betty by saying that she would get her gang to beat her up.

Betty ignored the girl for as long as she could. Her only hope was that one day she would be old enough to move away from the area and the girl. Suddenly she noticed an older girl walking in front of them. No one had noticed her before, but the older girl turned round and seemed angry. 'That's it!' she yelled. 'I've heard enough!' The older student said that if anyone touched Betty she would get her own gang to beat THEM up, and she explained that her gang was much bigger and went to the same school.

The student took Betty to one side and explained that her name was Margaret, and that she would always be around should Betty need help. Betty just nodded with her mouth open in shock. Someone believed in her. Someone stood up for her! Margaret turned around and said to the bully, 'You have been warned!' before walking away. Betty recalled that Margaret seemed to just vanish, and she never saw her again. She believes that Margaret was a guardian angel to her, but she didn't realise it until many years later. She had finally been saved from the horror that had plagued her every day of her life.

Walking home from school seems to be a pretty dangerous thing to do, as Lorraine also had a scary experience on her way home when she was nine years old. She found a match on the floor and says that curiosity got the better of her. She picked up the match and struck it. The flame touched her fingers, so she dropped it right away, but it was too late. Shockingly, the match fell into the pocket of the nylon dress she was wearing and Lorraine was in flames in seconds, not knowing what to do. She ran back to the schoolyard where a lady called Mrs White rolled her onto the grass and put out the flames.

Lorraine says that this woman was 'the angel who saved my life', but she doesn't believe she was the only one. Lorraine always felt she was in good hands. Even though she has some scarring on her legs, from the waist up she hasn't a single scar, which she believes is a miracle, particularly as she was running with the flames licking up both sides of her body. Doctors told her she could easily have been burned alive. She believes that her guardian angel was with her that day and protected her from far more serious damage, and even death. She says she shudders to think what would have happened if she had run home instead of back to school. That split-second decision seemed to be guided.

I remember messing around with a cap from a child's cap gun at a similar age. The little bits of paper were filled with powder, which would make a loud bang when struck with the toy gun, but they were also dangerous. I flicked one of the tiny charges with a pin one day and was trying (on purpose) to set light to a piece of paper with the spark it emitted. Kids can be so silly, right? The paper lit and I dropped it. The match immediately flew onto my legs, setting light to my school tights. I patted the flame with my hand and it went out, and I too was left unharmed. I had no scar at all and no pain from the flame. I was left terribly shocked, though, and I realised it served me right! I have to say that I never did anything so silly again, and warned friends and my younger sisters not to imitate my folly.

I recall another day when I was standing in the kitchen with my sisters, leaning against the cooker. I remember smelling burning, but had no idea what it was. I was wearing my thick school blazer and, unbeknown to me, the hob behind me was still switched on, though low. I had burned the sleeve of my jacket and the smell was terrible. It had melted and gone hard. Luckily for me it must have been fireproof in some way, because it hadn't burned through, and once again I was unharmed.

Was I just lucky in both cases, or was I being watched over and protected? I really feel that someone was keeping an eye out for me that day, and that it wasn't 'my time'.

Angels can sometimes bring warnings to parents and grandparents that their children are in trouble. This is what happened to another lady called Lorraine. She told me that when her son was just 12 days old she had a dream in which an angel was telling her to get help. Lorraine discovered that her baby was seriously ill, and when she rushed to the hospital she was told that her newborn had meningococcal septicaemia. The baby was very poorly but went on to recover, eventually coming home. He's now 27 but still has problems occasionally; his mum is grateful for the angelic warning.

It seems like the angels have never really left

Lorraine, even though she is not always aware of it. Her husband has informed her that when their son has a bout of illness she talks to people at the side of the bed when she is asleep! The anxious mum has no doubt she is chatting to the angels, receiving reassurance and continued advice from the other side.

Chapter 4

Love and Hugs

Roxanne was so sad when her family disapproved of her boyfriend. She was just 18 and her family asked her to leave the family home. As she says in her own words, she quickly became dependent on her relationship, even though it was clear to her that she was far too young and immature to be on her own without her family. It wasn't until four and a half years later that she felt ready to walk away from the relationship. She says that she just didn't feel any love from him. Hardest of all was missing a cuddle from someone who truly loved you.

Now broke and working full-time to pay off debts created by her ex-boyfriend, Roxanne was at least given a new flat to live in by the council. It was a small comfort. One afternoon she was sitting in the bathroom, her chest heaving from the power of her tears. She felt so sad. As she got up to walk out of the room she was suddenly stopped in her tracks. She felt as though her eyes were gently closed, and this was followed by a warm 'whooshing sensation'. A feeling of pure love surrounded her and it held her in place. As she took in a big breath, she felt the lovely feeling of huge wings around her, as if it had hit her very soul. Then it placed her back down very gently. She wasn't totally sure if she had been lifted up physically, but it felt like maybe her soul had been picked up as though it were a child and given a loving, snuggling hug!

That moment was certainly life-changing, and even now Roxanne says that she always talks to the angels and spirits when she feels the need, even if it's just to share her happiness about a special life moment. She mentioned that many of her friends call her 'weird' because of her beliefs in the angels, but from a young age she knew it was fine. Her nana also had experiences! Mine did, too, and I also don't mind being thought of as 'weird' (weird is good!).

She confided that her best friend was killed when he was 15, and when he came to visit her in a dream it was her first experience of 'something else' and it really cemented her belief. Strangely, I also had an old school friend visit me in a dream. He had died at a very young age (from cancer). I have written about this in an earlier book, but his visit helped me realise there was more to life, and it prompted my whole writing career! His visit to me was so clear and real that I knew after that moment that life goes on. I was so excited I wanted to share it with the world ... so I did!

From Angels with Love

I've also been lucky enough to have a spiritual hug. It's happened on numerous occasions. At times of great distress I've suddenly felt overwhelmed with love. The feeling was so powerful it made me cry uncontrollably. It was love like I had never felt. Then, almost as quickly as it had come, it just disappeared again! I felt at peace afterwards, relieved almost. It felt like I had been holding onto something (worry? Anger? Tension?), and after the experience of total, unconditional love, all the pain and the bodily aches simply melted away. It was pretty wonderful.

Over the years, I've run numerous angel workshops. As part of these I have sometimes held guided meditation sessions. What this means is that I have used my voice to take people on a mental 'journey'. That experience included me guiding them to meet their own guardian angel. During the meditation people often weep with joy at the feeling of love they experience as their guardian angel – their very own personal angel guide – fills them with a powerful energy. People don't always cry, of course, but I do remember one afternoon class where the whole group was in tears – this was the angels' influence, not mine, I might add. It was a very healing day! It's wonderful to feel their unconditional adoration for their human charges: us.

Does any of this feel familiar to you? Have you ever been hugged by an angel? It's very unlikely you

47

would have seen an angel (although as we have seen, some people do). But maybe you felt the sensation of an angelic hug – the weight of an arm around your shoulder or maybe an unseen hand holding tightly onto yours. You could have the feeling that your angel is standing behind you, with either arms (or wings) wrapping themselves comfortingly around you, or just knowing that you are somehow surrounded by a cloud or blanket of loving energy so strong that it almost blocks out everything else around you.

In that moment, the surrounding world seems to fade away and love becomes all that there is – or the ALL THAT IS (another phrase for God or the Source, our creator). Remember always that angels are God's messengers, his intermediaries between heaven and earth. The love that we feel may be brought via angels, but its origin is from a being much bigger than we can ever imagine.

When might you feel an angel's loving hug?

- During times of grief
- When you are under great emotional stress
- When you feel alone
- During times of danger
- When your life is under threat (maybe because you are ill or waiting for an operation, for example)

From Angels with Love

- When you feel overwhelmed or uncertain
- At times when you are fearful
- When you are very lonely
- Any time when you need reassurance that you are not alone and that, yes, you are also loved

When an angel is near you might experience one of the following:

- The scent of flowers
- The strong smell of vanilla
- A little light-headedness
- You might feel as if the world around you fades away (some people say the world seems to phase out, as if they were out of time momentarily)
- Tingling, buzzing or a vibration-like feeling
- A rapid heartbeat as the energy around you changes/speeds up (*Check with your doctor that this isn't a medical condition*)
- A powerful feeling of unconditional love
- Clouds of bright light that don't hurt your eyes
- Tiny dots of light flickering around you (*As above, if you are getting unusual eye activity, don't assume it's angels – for safety's sake, do get changes of light phenomena checked out by a medical professional to rule out eye damage first of all*)
- Coloured lights or rainbows
- Musical sounds (choir-like voices, music-box tinkling, bell tones)

- Unusual paranormal phenomena that don't (usually) frighten you. Lights flickering, TV switching on by itself, radio switching channel and so on (this can also be deceased loved ones trying to let you know they are okay and safe)
- One person told me they felt a warmth in their chest, pleasant and comforting
- Another described a 'cool, tingling, goosebump sensation'
- Suddenly and unexpectedly falling asleep, and having very real dreams of spirits/angels communicating with you
- Feeling as if something or someone is hugging you tightly in a warm embrace

As we have seen, this last interaction can be extremely powerful. One lady says that she hugs her angel right back. She lies on her side and stretches out her arms as if she were hugging someone. She senses that her guardian angel comes to her side. (You could use a pillow as an angel substitute to help things along a little!) Another lady said that she would regularly wake up with a blissful feeling and a tingle around her head, and would literally feel as if she were being hugged (she said it felt nothing like a muscle spasm, which someone had rudely suggested it might be!).

Sometimes the hug is visual. People tell me about little lights they see around them, or a strange white mist! This can even be photographed. After losing someone close, it's not uncommon for a mist to appear around another person in a photograph, almost as if the lost love wanted to jump into the photo, too, and let you know they were still around. I've seen photographs with mists visible that look like loving arms around someone's shoulder, and even an 'angel-type' wing appear in shot! Have you ever seen photographs of your own that look like this?

One little girl was seriously ill; there was no hope for recovery. Every day she would see the angels in her bedroom and point them out to her parents. Her mum and dad could not see them, but she described the angels in great detail; each one had different-coloured hair.

One day in hospital, her parents knew their little one wouldn't be coming home with them again. It was her time. The youngster pointed out the angels again – they had gathered in her room. This time they were not alone. 'Can you see Jesus, Mummy?' the young girl asked. Jesus was standing with his arms outstretched in welcome. He was ready to hug this little one and take her home to heaven, and the little girl told her parents she was now so tired that she had decided to go with him. Her mum and dad were devastated when their little one passed away later that day, but knowing that Jesus and the angels were holding out their arms in welcome made it just a little easier.

Another couple were devastated after the sudden loss of their own youngster. That night as they lay in their bed, both completely shocked, they were surrounded by a sudden feeling of peace and warmth. It was as if the angels themselves had reached down to reassure them that their daughter was safe. The mum wrote that she literally cried with joy at this amazing feeling, and they both fell into a deep sleep, ready to face the challenging days ahead.

Nothing can ever take away these losses, but it's nice to know that the soul continues to exist and is safe with the angels. Somehow, some way – in a way we don't totally understand – our loved ones continue to live in another dimension and another existence. So many people have these experiences, so many feel and sense an angel's presence and their love. Many witness Jesus and other religious figures, or feel the peace and affection that seems to come from God himself. It helps people to cope during the darkest of days.

Claire felt that she received an angel hug, too. She told me that a few years back she was so distressed one day that she was crying and couldn't seem to stop. At the time, she told me, she was lying down and felt someone lie at her side. Claire was very surprised, but as she turned around she saw what she described as an angel. It was as if the angel had come to comfort her. What a blessing to be able to see with her physical eyes that which so many do not! In an instant she had a feeling of extreme peace and calmness wash over her. She was literally hugged by an angel, in a visit of comfort and joy. I love that story!

After my own dad passed away many years ago, my mum woke up one day knowing that Dad's spirit had been in bed hugging her all night. She actually felt the sensation, and when she awoke she was momentarily confused that he wasn't still there. The strange thing was that it wasn't even in the house they had shared together. Mum was visiting a relative and it was the first time she had slept in a double bed since Dad had passed away, but it didn't make a difference to Dad. He found her anyway – and took advantage of the extra space in the bed! It's comforting, isn't it, to know that our loved ones can track us down wherever we are? It's the vibration of the love we shared in life that acts as a sort of satellite navigation system in death ... or a 'satnav' as we call it in our house!

Katya also had a reassuring hug when she needed it most. She explained that many years ago her husband was in intensive care, fighting for his life. He'd been transferred to a hospital for specialist treatment, which was miles away from home, so Katya was offered accommodation in the nearby nurses' quarters, keeping her close to her sick husband. The young woman was scared, alone and petrified of losing her 36-year-old husband, the father of their two very young boys. Yet that night,

Jacky Newcomb

as she lay in bed, she says something enveloped her – a 'beyond beautiful' being of light engulfed her, and the feeling of love and reassurance was overwhelming. For the first time since her husband had become ill she felt calm, and from then on Katya says she knew that everything would be okay.

There is an extra little something to this story. She tells me that this experience happened nine years ago. Her husband is now fit and healthy and they've added a little girl to their 'collection'! Wonderful news indeed!

Julia confided that after a massive argument with her husband she was so upset she went downstairs and sat on the sofa in tears. It was then that she felt an invisible arm go around her shoulder and hug her tightly! The experience brought her 'all the joy of pure love and peace', and she says it was the most amazing experience. Surely one she won't forget in a hurry.

A lady called Debbie was scared about an operation she had coming up. She told me that she prayed for the strength to get through the ordeal. 'From the minute I left my house to when it was over I felt a loving warmth around my shoulders,' she explained. 'It was amazing, and I got through the operation just fine.' How wonderful to feel comfort like this before a medical procedure. So many people are scared at this time, and lots of people share their angel experiences relating to illness and hospital visits.

Lynn was also in hospital when her angels came to call. She explained that at the time she was in a lot of pain, but she suddenly felt an arm around her shoulder. At first she thought it was a nurse, but when she opened her eyes to look she witnessed an angel. The being told her, 'Everything will be all right, you are going to be fine.' Lynn felt calm, closed her eyes and relaxed as a warm, glowing energy swept through her body. The pain immediately eased and as she opened her eyes to say thanks, she realised the angel had disappeared. Lynn told me that she has never forgotten the amazing feeing, and I know she was very grateful.

A different Lynne also felt a hand upon her shoulder when she was going through a stressful time. She says the hand felt small and cool. And when Kerry's son tragically died and she was sobbing with grief, she told me that she felt a tapping on her shoulder, as if someone were trying to comfort her and let her know she was not alone.

When angels came to visit Jo it helped her to realise that there was more to life than we know. She told me that she was very upset about something one day and felt that she really needed someone to be with her to comfort her. It was at that very moment that Jo felt two arms wrap around her from behind. Although she was surprised, she was not afraid. The embrace was full of love, she told me, and it stayed with her until she felt better.

Jacky Newcomb

Another lady explained how she felt her angel's hand on her shoulder when she was in hospital last year. It instantly calmed her, in exactly the same way that it did with all the other people who have shared their amazing experiences. This is just a small selection of the many angel-hug stories I've been told over the years. Their aim is clear: they, the angelic realm, aim to comfort, calm and reassure us. If these examples are anything to go by, it certainly works. Have you ever been hugged by an angel?

Chapter 5

The Little Ways They Send Us Love

The interaction with an angel may well be dramatic, but their contact, as we have seen, takes many forms. A spirit visited my sister recently while she slept. The spirit wanted her to pass on a message to others he had been unable to reach. He said he would make his presence known by bringing them feelings that he was around, and also by making noises. This actually set off alarm bells for me! Hearing a sound with no obvious source is not really one of the more gentle ways that angels and spirits could reach out to us.

Let's face it, if you hear a sound in another room and you are alone in the house, your first thought isn't going to be, *Oh, it's an angel*, or, *Ah, it's just Uncle Bill* …! I know if it were me, I would probably think we had burglars, or maybe that the cat had knocked something over. If it were night-time you might even wonder if you had a ghost in the house! I hope this loving spirit is gentle with his grieving family.

Jacky Newcomb

Many of my readers want their angels and spiritual guides to make their presence known in a more obvious way, but trust me, you really don't! I can't imagine anything worse than being scared half to death by these loving beings. I've been in this business many years and nothing much scares me, but still … I prefer my angels to visit in dreams or to leave me little white feathers or coins (angelic calling cards). On a bright, sunny day I'm not against having a little fun. Objects appearing without any obvious person putting them there or the TV switching on by itself don't scare me – but I appreciate that they might frighten you.

If you'd like a sign, it's okay to ask for one. It's also okay to ask the angels to bring a subtle sign or to indicate the type of sign that would be acceptable to you. Asking angels (or deceased loved ones) to flicker lights when you are not alone might be just fine! Graeme wrote to explain how he had done exactly that. He says he was reading my book, *An Angel Held My Hand*, and one story in particular made him wonder if he could receive some sort of sign from an angel if he simply asked for one. Later in the day, when this was furthest from his mind, he was on his way out of the front door when a single white feather floated down and landed at his feet in the middle of the porch. Graeme told me that he feels sure this was the angelic sign he'd requested earlier in the day.

Here are some more of your lovely experiences.

From Angels with Love

Irene tells me that although she hasn't seen an angel, she does feel their presence around her. Mary is a spiritual lady and she felt an angel place its hand on her shoulder while she was having a healing session. She explained that as this happened she could smell the distinct aroma of vanilla around her, and it felt like someone was sitting on her feet (not too heavily, I hope!). She tells me that it was very comforting. Notice how these same phrases come up again and again?

Then Neen contacted me to explain that there is an angel she works with regularly. He lifts her head up, gently pushes her shoulders back and helps her literally keep her chin up, she tells me. She is writing a book about her experiences but says it was during a 'Meet Your Guardian Angel' meditation that she played on a CD (one of my own angel meditations) that she first saw the angel. She told me, 'I went into a temple of light and saw him stood there. I said to him, "You?" and he said, "Yes, are you okay with that?"' Of course she was, and she has felt the angel with her every day since that time. She feels he has helped her so much. Isn't it strange that when she came face to face with her angel she recognised him?

Ruth feels angels around her all the time, and Gilli saw an archangel at a funeral. She explained how she had asked the Archangel Raphael to help the grieving family after she felt the presence of the deceased man request it. It was then that she saw

Raphael standing behind the wife and children. He wrapped his wings around them in a comforting embrace.

Nicola felt an unmistakeable hand upon her shoulder while she was walking through the beautiful grounds of her local stately home. She admits that she doesn't know if it was an angel or not, but as she turned around there was no one there who could have touched her. The experience didn't startle her, but it was certainly a little confusing!

Jennette had an angel place their hand on her right shoulder when she was about 20 years old. The young woman was driving her first car and backing out of a blind parking spot at the time. She also heard the word 'Wait', so she stopped immediately. In following this advice, Jennette avoided a collision with a car that drove past at that very moment. She feels that if they hadn't warned her, the consequences could have been catastrophic. She's never forgotten it and says she never will. Was it an angel? She remembers seeing a white hand and had the feeling that the energy was male. How wonderful to have a driving angel!

Jelena had an unusual experience. Was it an angel, or someone sent by angels? She explained how one day she had buried something important under a tree in a nearby wood to keep it safe from someone. After a while she needed the object back, so she went to dig it up again. Looking at all the trees, she panicked a little as she couldn't remember exactly which one she had used.

Eventually Jelena selected the most likely tree, but after half an hour of digging the object hadn't appeared. Distressed, she started to cry and asked her guardian angel to help her. Shortly afterwards, a man passed by and said to her, 'Hey, girl, don't dig under that walnut tree, that soil is not good for flowers.' She thanked the man and, smiling now, she immediately realised her mistake and felt guided to a tree right next to the one she had been digging under. It was almost as if the message had a double meaning. It was certainly perfectly timed. This time Jelena found her object instantly. Isn't that strange?

She also had another experience that she shared with me. It's one of the 'spirit photographs' we talked about earlier. After ending a short romance, Jelena felt sad and asked her guardian angel for a sign that she would be okay; she was simply looking for a little comfort. That weekend she went on a short trip with some friends where they visited some waterfalls and took photographs of the occasion. Later, when she put the photographs onto her computer, she spotted something behind her in the waterfall. The water appeared to have created the shape of an angel putting its hand upon her right shoulder! Isn't that lovely?

Michel's experience came more as a feeling. He explained that he was driving and feeling down when all of a sudden he had the sensation of being wrapped in love. He asked, 'What is this?' and started to laugh. It was the first time he'd ever had an experience of this type but confesses he hasn't felt it again since. He admits that it's amazing to feel love like that, a real blessing.

Elizabeth's angel was her dad. She was just nine years old when he appeared to her as a spirit. She was staring at the wall and when her mum and sisters asked her why, she explained that she could see her dad. Later that very same day she felt him kiss her goodnight as she lay in bed. Love is such a powerful emotion – it seems to pass all boundaries of time and space, doesn't it?

When Janice's mum passed away, she felt that she had also lost her best friend. They were very close. A year after her passing, the family all went on holiday to France together, taking Janice's father with them. One day Janice was sitting in the back of the car, looking out of the side window, when she asked her mum to give her a sign that she was with them. Moments later a beautiful heart-shaped cloud appeared in the sky. It was lit from behind by a very bright light, and Janice feels sure that the heart was her sign. I'm sure it was!

Debora explained how she was very worried about the health of a loved one and at the time she kept asking for help and support to comfort him. A few days later she got a reply. Debora posted me a photograph of a cloud in the shape of an angel! She said, 'To me, it was a sign that they were working on it.' Thankfully the diagnosis was better than had been expected, and Debora says she was so thankful for the angels' help and support during a stressful time in her life.

Kerry was also going through a very overwhelming time when she had her experience. She used to lie down at night and worry about the issues in her life before falling asleep. But then, she explained, she'd hear the sound of harmonious singing all around her. Kerry says she couldn't hear any words because the beautiful voices emitted more of a hum; it sounded like a choir. She admitted that at first she would be scared of this unexplained sound, but eventually the tones calmed her. The overall experience made Kerry feel protected.

On another occasion she recalls lying on her bed feeling unwell when she felt a kiss on her cheek. No one else was in the room at the time. Kerry was pregnant and the following morning she had a massive haemorrhage. Thankfully, both she and the baby lived, so it makes you wonder – had an angel come to tell Kerry that she was not going to be alone during her ordeal?

Angels are the most wonderful beings of light. They have interacted with humankind since the beginning of time. There are millions of stories of their interactions with us. Many religions teach that we each have our own guardian angel. Angels are assigned to us at birth and watch over us every day. Your angel brings you total and unconditional love, and I hope you get the opportunity to feel the presence of your own angelic guardian.

Some of the most wonderful experiences have happened to people after they have invited angels to be part of their lives. You don't need any fancy equipment to do this. If you've read any of my other books about angels you will know that the simplest way to do this is to ask them. You can write to them, chat to them in your mind or speak aloud. Your angel is always there for you and you can request help with anything that is important to you. They can assist you in many ways – no problem is too big or too small for them to handle. In your mind you can ask them:

> Loving angels, I'd love more signs that you are part of my life.
> I ask that you step forward when I'm sad, lonely or frightened.
> I invite you into my life.

As you speak these words, you might hear your angel reply to you:

From Angels with Love

Dear one, we are always here.
We, your loving angels, are always at your side.
It will be our pleasure to communicate with you.

♥

My dear readers,

It has been the greatest of pleasures to compile this book for you. If you've enjoyed reading about your loving guardian angels, be sure to check out the other books in this series for more magical, true-life angel experiences.

If you'd like more information about angels then you can visit my website: www.JackyNewcomb.com. You'll also find me on Facebook and Twitter if you'd like to communicate with me directly. And of course it goes without saying that I'd love to hear about your own angelic encounters.

Until next time then ...
Angel blessings,
Jacky Newcomb

www.JackyNewcomb.com

From Angels with Love

Dear one, we are always here.
We watch, waiting to guide you wherever you walk.
It will be our pleasure to reveal more when we...

My dear readers,

It has been the greatest of pleasures to compile this book for you. If you've enjoyed reading about your Earthly guardian angels, be sure to check out the other books in this series for more on angels, and on angelic encounters.

If you'd like more information about angels, then you can visit my website: www.JackyNewcomb.com. You'll also find me on Facebook and Twitter if you'd like to communicate with me directly. And of course it goes without saying that I'd love to hear about your own angelic encounters.

Until next time then...
Angel blessings,
Jacky Newcomb

www.JackyNewcomb.com

Harper True.

Time to be inspired

Write for us

Do you have a true life story of your own?

Whether you think it will inspire us, move us, make us laugh or make us cry, we want to hear from you.

To find out more, visit

www.harpertrue.com or send your ideas to harpertrue@harpercollins.co.uk and soon you could be a published author.